Staying Organized, Detailed and On Time

A Notes Weekly Planner

Activinotes

DAILY JOURNALS, PLANNERS, NOTEBOOKS AND OTHER BLANK BOOKS

PLAN YOUR WORK THEN WORK YOUR PLAN

MONDAY

9:00 AM	4:00 PM
10:00 AM	5:00 PM
11:00 AM	6:00 PM
12:00 PM	MUST DOs
1:00 PM	☐
2:00 PM	☐
3:00 PM	☐

TUESDAY

9:00 AM	4:00 PM
10:00 AM	5:00 PM
11:00 AM	6:00 PM
12:00 PM	MUST DOs
1:00 PM	☐
2:00 PM	☐
3:00 PM	☐

WEDNESDAY

9:00 AM	4:00 PM
10:00 AM	5:00 PM
11:00 AM	6:00 PM
12:00 PM	MUST DOs
1:00 PM	☐
2:00 PM	☐
3:00 PM	☐

THURSDAY

9:00 AM	4:00 PM
10:00 AM	5:00 PM
11:00 AM	6:00 PM
12:00 PM	MUST DOs
1:00 PM	☐
2:00 PM	☐
3:00 PM	☐

FRIDAY

9:00 AM	4:00 PM
10:00 AM	5:00 PM
11:00 AM	6:00 PM
12:00 PM	MUST DOs
1:00 PM	☐
2:00 PM	☐
3:00 PM	☐

SATURDAY
APPOINTMENTS

SUNDAY
APPOINTMENTS

MUST DOs

☐

☐

MUST DOs

☐

☐

Weekly Planner

Date: _____

TO DO	SPECIAL EVENT

APPOINTMENTS	THINGS TO BUY

REMINDERS	NEED TO CALL

REMARKS

MONDAY

9:00 AM	4:00 PM
10:00 AM	5:00 PM
11:00 AM	6:00 PM
12:00 PM	MUST DOs
1:00 PM	☐
2:00 PM	☐
3:00 PM	☐

TUESDAY

9:00 AM	4:00 PM
10:00 AM	5:00 PM
11:00 AM	6:00 PM
12:00 PM	MUST DOs
1:00 PM	☐
2:00 PM	☐
3:00 PM	☐

WEDNESDAY

9:00 AM	4:00 PM
10:00 AM	5:00 PM
11:00 AM	6:00 PM
12:00 PM	MUST DOs
1:00 PM	☐
2:00 PM	☐
3:00 PM	☐

THURSDAY

9:00 AM	4:00 PM
10:00 AM	5:00 PM
11:00 AM	6:00 PM
12:00 PM	MUST DOs
1:00 PM	☐
2:00 PM	☐
3:00 PM	☐

FRIDAY

9:00 AM	4:00 PM
10:00 AM	5:00 PM
11:00 AM	6:00 PM
12:00 PM	MUST DOs
1:00 PM	☐
2:00 PM	☐
3:00 PM	☐

SATURDAY
APPOINTMENTS

MUST DOs
☐
☐

SUNDAY
APPOINTMENTS

MUST DOs
☐
☐

Weekly Planner
Date: _____

TO DO	SPECIAL EVENT

APPOINTMENTS	THINGS TO BUY

REMINDERS	NEED TO CALL

REMARKS

MONDAY

9:00 AM	4:00 PM
10:00 AM	5:00 PM
11:00 AM	6:00 PM
12:00 PM	MUST DOs
1:00 PM	☐
2:00 PM	☐
3:00 PM	☐

TUESDAY

9:00 AM	4:00 PM
10:00 AM	5:00 PM
11:00 AM	6:00 PM
12:00 PM	MUST DOs
1:00 PM	☐
2:00 PM	☐
3:00 PM	☐

WEDNESDAY

9:00 AM	4:00 PM
10:00 AM	5:00 PM
11:00 AM	6:00 PM
12:00 PM	MUST DOs
1:00 PM	☐
2:00 PM	☐
3:00 PM	☐

THURSDAY

9:00 AM	4:00 PM
10:00 AM	5:00 PM
11:00 AM	6:00 PM
12:00 PM	MUST DOs
1:00 PM	☐
2:00 PM	☐
3:00 PM	☐

FRIDAY

9:00 AM	4:00 PM
10:00 AM	5:00 PM
11:00 AM	6:00 PM
12:00 PM	MUST DOs
1:00 PM	☐
2:00 PM	☐
3:00 PM	☐

SATURDAY
APPOINTMENTS

SUNDAY
APPOINTMENTS

MUST DOs
☐
☐

MUST DOs
☐
☐

Weekly Planner
Date: _____

TO DO

SPECIAL EVENT

APPOINTMENTS

THINGS TO BUY

REMINDERS

NEED TO CALL

REMARKS

MONDAY

9:00 AM	4:00 PM
10:00 AM	5:00 PM
11:00 AM	6:00 PM
12:00 PM	MUST DOs
1:00 PM	☐
2:00 PM	☐
3:00 PM	☐

TUESDAY

9:00 AM	4:00 PM
10:00 AM	5:00 PM
11:00 AM	6:00 PM
12:00 PM	MUST DOs
1:00 PM	☐
2:00 PM	☐
3:00 PM	☐

WEDNESDAY

9:00 AM	4:00 PM
10:00 AM	5:00 PM
11:00 AM	6:00 PM
12:00 PM	MUST DOs
1:00 PM	☐
2:00 PM	☐
3:00 PM	☐

THURSDAY

9:00 AM	4:00 PM
10:00 AM	5:00 PM
11:00 AM	6:00 PM
12:00 PM	MUST DOs
1:00 PM	☐
2:00 PM	☐
3:00 PM	☐

FRIDAY

9:00 AM	4:00 PM
10:00 AM	5:00 PM
11:00 AM	6:00 PM
12:00 PM	MUST DOs
1:00 PM	☐
2:00 PM	☐
3:00 PM	☐

SATURDAY
APPOINTMENTS

_____

_____

_____

MUST DOs

☐

☐

SUNDAY
APPOINTMENTS

_____

_____

_____

MUST DOs

☐

☐

Weekly Planner

Date: _____

TO DO	SPECIAL EVENT

APPOINTMENTS	THINGS TO BUY

REMINDERS	NEED TO CALL

REMARKS

MONDAY

9:00 AM	4:00 PM
10:00 AM	5:00 PM
11:00 AM	6:00 PM
12:00 PM	MUST DOs
1:00 PM	☐
2:00 PM	☐
3:00 PM	☐

TUESDAY

9:00 AM	4:00 PM
10:00 AM	5:00 PM
11:00 AM	6:00 PM
12:00 PM	MUST DOs
1:00 PM	☐
2:00 PM	☐
3:00 PM	☐

WEDNESDAY

9:00 AM	4:00 PM
10:00 AM	5:00 PM
11:00 AM	6:00 PM
12:00 PM	MUST DOs
1:00 PM	☐
2:00 PM	☐
3:00 PM	☐

THURSDAY

9:00 AM	4:00 PM
10:00 AM	5:00 PM
11:00 AM	6:00 PM
12:00 PM	MUST DOs
1:00 PM	☐
2:00 PM	☐
3:00 PM	☐

FRIDAY

9:00 AM	4:00 PM
10:00 AM	5:00 PM
11:00 AM	6:00 PM
12:00 PM	MUST DOs
1:00 PM	☐
2:00 PM	☐
3:00 PM	☐

SATURDAY
APPOINTMENTS

SUNDAY
APPOINTMENTS

MUST DOs	MUST DOs
☐	☐
☐	☐

Weekly Planner
Date: _____

TO DO

SPECIAL EVENT

APPOINTMENTS

THINGS TO BUY

REMINDERS

NEED TO CALL

REMARKS

MONDAY

9:00 AM	4:00 PM
10:00 AM	5:00 PM
11:00 AM	6:00 PM
12:00 PM	MUST DOs
1:00 PM	☐
2:00 PM	☐
3:00 PM	☐

TUESDAY

9:00 AM	4:00 PM
10:00 AM	5:00 PM
11:00 AM	6:00 PM
12:00 PM	MUST DOs
1:00 PM	☐
2:00 PM	☐
3:00 PM	☐

WEDNESDAY

9:00 AM	4:00 PM
10:00 AM	5:00 PM
11:00 AM	6:00 PM
12:00 PM	MUST DOs
1:00 PM	☐
2:00 PM	☐
3:00 PM	☐

THURSDAY

9:00 AM	4:00 PM
10:00 AM	5:00 PM
11:00 AM	6:00 PM
12:00 PM	MUST DOs
1:00 PM	☐
2:00 PM	☐
3:00 PM	☐

FRIDAY

9:00 AM	4:00 PM
10:00 AM	5:00 PM
11:00 AM	6:00 PM
12:00 PM	MUST DOs
1:00 PM	☐
2:00 PM	☐
3:00 PM	☐

SATURDAY
APPOINTMENTS

SUNDAY
APPOINTMENTS

MUST DOs

☐

☐

MUST DOs

☐

☐

Weekly Planner
Date: _____

TO DO	SPECIAL EVENT

APPOINTMENTS	THINGS TO BUY

REMINDERS	NEED TO CALL

REMARKS

MONDAY

9:00 AM	4:00 PM
10:00 AM	5:00 PM
11:00 AM	6:00 PM
12:00 PM	MUST DOs
1:00 PM	☐
2:00 PM	☐
3:00 PM	☐

TUESDAY

9:00 AM	4:00 PM
10:00 AM	5:00 PM
11:00 AM	6:00 PM
12:00 PM	MUST DOs
1:00 PM	☐
2:00 PM	☐
3:00 PM	☐

WEDNESDAY

9:00 AM	4:00 PM
10:00 AM	5:00 PM
11:00 AM	6:00 PM
12:00 PM	MUST DOs
1:00 PM	☐
2:00 PM	☐
3:00 PM	☐

THURSDAY

9:00 AM	4:00 PM
10:00 AM	5:00 PM
11:00 AM	6:00 PM
12:00 PM	MUST DOs
1:00 PM	☐
2:00 PM	☐
3:00 PM	☐

FRIDAY

9:00 AM	4:00 PM
10:00 AM	5:00 PM
11:00 AM	6:00 PM
12:00 PM	MUST DOs
1:00 PM	☐
2:00 PM	☐
3:00 PM	☐

SATURDAY
APPOINTMENTS

SUNDAY
APPOINTMENTS

MUST DOs

☐

☐

MUST DOs

☐

☐

Weekly Planner

Date: _____

TO DO

SPECIAL EVENT

APPOINTMENTS

THINGS TO BUY

REMINDERS

NEED TO CALL

REMARKS

MONDAY

9:00 AM	4:00 PM
10:00 AM	5:00 PM
11:00 AM	6:00 PM
12:00 PM	MUST DOs
1:00 PM	☐
2:00 PM	☐
3:00 PM	☐

TUESDAY

9:00 AM	4:00 PM
10:00 AM	5:00 PM
11:00 AM	6:00 PM
12:00 PM	MUST DOs
1:00 PM	☐
2:00 PM	☐
3:00 PM	☐

WEDNESDAY

9:00 AM	4:00 PM
10:00 AM	5:00 PM
11:00 AM	6:00 PM
12:00 PM	MUST DOs
1:00 PM	☐
2:00 PM	☐
3:00 PM	☐

THURSDAY

9:00 AM	4:00 PM
10:00 AM	5:00 PM
11:00 AM	6:00 PM
12:00 PM	MUST DOs
1:00 PM	☐
2:00 PM	☐
3:00 PM	☐

FRIDAY

9:00 AM	4:00 PM
10:00 AM	5:00 PM
11:00 AM	6:00 PM
12:00 PM	MUST DOs
1:00 PM	☐
2:00 PM	☐
3:00 PM	☐

SATURDAY

APPOINTMENTS

SUNDAY

APPOINTMENTS

MUST DOs

☐

☐

MUST DOs

☐

☐

Weekly Planner

Date: _____

TO DO

SPECIAL EVENT

APPOINTMENTS

THINGS TO BUY

REMINDERS

NEED TO CALL

REMARKS

MONDAY

9:00 AM	4:00 PM
10:00 AM	5:00 PM
11:00 AM	6:00 PM
12:00 PM	MUST DOs
1:00 PM	☐
2:00 PM	☐
3:00 PM	☐

TUESDAY

9:00 AM	4:00 PM
10:00 AM	5:00 PM
11:00 AM	6:00 PM
12:00 PM	MUST DOs
1:00 PM	☐
2:00 PM	☐
3:00 PM	☐

WEDNESDAY

9:00 AM	4:00 PM
10:00 AM	5:00 PM
11:00 AM	6:00 PM
12:00 PM	MUST DOs
1:00 PM	☐
2:00 PM	☐
3:00 PM	☐

THURSDAY

9:00 AM	4:00 PM
10:00 AM	5:00 PM
11:00 AM	6:00 PM
12:00 PM	MUST DOs
1:00 PM	☐
2:00 PM	☐
3:00 PM	☐

FRIDAY

9:00 AM	4:00 PM
10:00 AM	5:00 PM
11:00 AM	6:00 PM
12:00 PM	MUST DOs
1:00 PM	☐
2:00 PM	☐
3:00 PM	☐

SATURDAY
APPOINTMENTS

SUNDAY
APPOINTMENTS

MUST DOs

☐
☐

MUST DOs

☐
☐

Weekly Planner

Date: _____

TO DO	SPECIAL EVENT

APPOINTMENTS	THINGS TO BUY

REMINDERS	NEED TO CALL

REMARKS

MONDAY

9:00 AM	4:00 PM
10:00 AM	5:00 PM
11:00 AM	6:00 PM
12:00 PM	MUST DOs
1:00 PM	☐
2:00 PM	☐
3:00 PM	☐

TUESDAY

9:00 AM	4:00 PM
10:00 AM	5:00 PM
11:00 AM	6:00 PM
12:00 PM	MUST DOs
1:00 PM	☐
2:00 PM	☐
3:00 PM	☐

WEDNESDAY

9:00 AM	4:00 PM
10:00 AM	5:00 PM
11:00 AM	6:00 PM
12:00 PM	MUST DOs
1:00 PM	☐
2:00 PM	☐
3:00 PM	☐

THURSDAY

9:00 AM	4:00 PM
10:00 AM	5:00 PM
11:00 AM	6:00 PM
12:00 PM	MUST DOs
1:00 PM	☐
2:00 PM	☐
3:00 PM	☐

FRIDAY

9:00 AM	4:00 PM
10:00 AM	5:00 PM
11:00 AM	6:00 PM
12:00 PM	MUST DOs
1:00 PM	☐
2:00 PM	☐
3:00 PM	☐

SATURDAY
APPOINTMENTS

SUNDAY
APPOINTMENTS

MUST DOs

☐

☐

MUST DOs

☐

☐

Weekly Planner

Date: _____

TO DO

SPECIAL EVENT

APPOINTMENTS

THINGS TO BUY

REMINDERS

NEED TO CALL

REMARKS

MONDAY

9:00 AM	4:00 PM
10:00 AM	5:00 PM
11:00 AM	6:00 PM
12:00 PM	MUST DOs
1:00 PM	☐
2:00 PM	☐
3:00 PM	☐

TUESDAY

9:00 AM	4:00 PM
10:00 AM	5:00 PM
11:00 AM	6:00 PM
12:00 PM	MUST DOs
1:00 PM	☐
2:00 PM	☐
3:00 PM	☐

WEDNESDAY

9:00 AM	4:00 PM
10:00 AM	5:00 PM
11:00 AM	6:00 PM
12:00 PM	MUST DOs
1:00 PM	☐
2:00 PM	☐
3:00 PM	☐

THURSDAY

9:00 AM	4:00 PM
10:00 AM	5:00 PM
11:00 AM	6:00 PM
12:00 PM	MUST DOs
1:00 PM	☐
2:00 PM	☐
3:00 PM	☐

FRIDAY

9:00 AM	4:00 PM
10:00 AM	5:00 PM
11:00 AM	6:00 PM
12:00 PM	MUST DOs
1:00 PM	☐
2:00 PM	☐
3:00 PM	☐

SATURDAY

APPOINTMENTS

MUST DOs

☐

☐

SUNDAY

APPOINTMENTS

MUST DOs

☐

☐

Weekly Planner
Date: _____

TO DO	SPECIAL EVENT

APPOINTMENTS	THINGS TO BUY

REMINDERS	NEED TO CALL

REMARKS

MONDAY

9:00 AM	4:00 PM
10:00 AM	5:00 PM
11:00 AM	6:00 PM
12:00 PM	MUST DOs
1:00 PM	☐
2:00 PM	☐
3:00 PM	☐

TUESDAY

9:00 AM	4:00 PM
10:00 AM	5:00 PM
11:00 AM	6:00 PM
12:00 PM	MUST DOs
1:00 PM	☐
2:00 PM	☐
3:00 PM	☐

WEDNESDAY

9:00 AM	4:00 PM
10:00 AM	5:00 PM
11:00 AM	6:00 PM
12:00 PM	MUST DOs
1:00 PM	☐
2:00 PM	☐
3:00 PM	☐

THURSDAY

9:00 AM	4:00 PM
10:00 AM	5:00 PM
11:00 AM	6:00 PM
12:00 PM	MUST DOs
1:00 PM	☐
2:00 PM	☐
3:00 PM	☐

FRIDAY

9:00 AM	4:00 PM
10:00 AM	5:00 PM
11:00 AM	6:00 PM
12:00 PM	MUST DOs
1:00 PM	☐
2:00 PM	☐
3:00 PM	☐

SATURDAY
APPOINTMENTS

_____

_____

_____

MUST DOs

☐

☐

SUNDAY
APPOINTMENTS

_____

_____

_____

MUST DOs

☐

☐

Weekly Planner

Date: _____

TO DO	SPECIAL EVENT

APPOINTMENTS	THINGS TO BUY

REMINDERS	NEED TO CALL

REMARKS

MONDAY

9:00 AM	4:00 PM
10:00 AM	5:00 PM
11:00 AM	6:00 PM
12:00 PM	MUST DOs
1:00 PM	☐
2:00 PM	☐
3:00 PM	☐

TUESDAY

9:00 AM	4:00 PM
10:00 AM	5:00 PM
11:00 AM	6:00 PM
12:00 PM	MUST DOs
1:00 PM	☐
2:00 PM	☐
3:00 PM	☐

WEDNESDAY

9:00 AM	4:00 PM
10:00 AM	5:00 PM
11:00 AM	6:00 PM
12:00 PM	MUST DOs
1:00 PM	☐
2:00 PM	☐
3:00 PM	☐

THURSDAY

9:00 AM	4:00 PM
10:00 AM	5:00 PM
11:00 AM	6:00 PM
12:00 PM	MUST DOs
1:00 PM	☐
2:00 PM	☐
3:00 PM	☐

FRIDAY

9:00 AM	4:00 PM
10:00 AM	5:00 PM
11:00 AM	6:00 PM
12:00 PM	MUST DOs
1:00 PM	☐
2:00 PM	☐
3:00 PM	☐

SATURDAY

APPOINTMENTS

SUNDAY

APPOINTMENTS

MUST DOs

☐
☐

MUST DOs

☐
☐

Weekly Planner

Date: _____

TO DO

SPECIAL EVENT

APPOINTMENTS

THINGS TO BUY

REMINDERS

NEED TO CALL

REMARKS

MONDAY

9:00 AM	4:00 PM
10:00 AM	5:00 PM
11:00 AM	6:00 PM
12:00 PM	MUST DOs
1:00 PM	☐
2:00 PM	☐
3:00 PM	☐

TUESDAY

9:00 AM	4:00 PM
10:00 AM	5:00 PM
11:00 AM	6:00 PM
12:00 PM	MUST DOs
1:00 PM	☐
2:00 PM	☐
3:00 PM	☐

WEDNESDAY

9:00 AM	4:00 PM
10:00 AM	5:00 PM
11:00 AM	6:00 PM
12:00 PM	MUST DOs
1:00 PM	☐
2:00 PM	☐
3:00 PM	☐

THURSDAY

9:00 AM	4:00 PM
10:00 AM	5:00 PM
11:00 AM	6:00 PM
12:00 PM	MUST DOs
1:00 PM	☐
2:00 PM	☐
3:00 PM	☐

FRIDAY

9:00 AM	4:00 PM
10:00 AM	5:00 PM
11:00 AM	6:00 PM
12:00 PM	MUST DOs
1:00 PM	☐
2:00 PM	☐
3:00 PM	☐

SATURDAY
APPOINTMENTS

SUNDAY
APPOINTMENTS

MUST DOs

☐

☐

MUST DOs

☐

☐

Weekly Planner

Date: _____

TO DO	SPECIAL EVENT

APPOINTMENTS	THINGS TO BUY

REMINDERS	NEED TO CALL

REMARKS

MONDAY

9:00 AM	4:00 PM
10:00 AM	5:00 PM
11:00 AM	6:00 PM
12:00 PM	MUST DOs
1:00 PM	☐
2:00 PM	☐
3:00 PM	☐

TUESDAY

9:00 AM	4:00 PM
10:00 AM	5:00 PM
11:00 AM	6:00 PM
12:00 PM	MUST DOs
1:00 PM	☐
2:00 PM	☐
3:00 PM	☐

WEDNESDAY

9:00 AM	4:00 PM
10:00 AM	5:00 PM
11:00 AM	6:00 PM
12:00 PM	MUST DOs
1:00 PM	☐
2:00 PM	☐
3:00 PM	☐

THURSDAY

9:00 AM	4:00 PM
10:00 AM	5:00 PM
11:00 AM	6:00 PM
12:00 PM	MUST DOs
1:00 PM	☐
2:00 PM	☐
3:00 PM	☐

FRIDAY

9:00 AM	4:00 PM
10:00 AM	5:00 PM
11:00 AM	6:00 PM
12:00 PM	MUST DOs
1:00 PM	☐
2:00 PM	☐
3:00 PM	☐

SATURDAY
APPOINTMENTS

SUNDAY
APPOINTMENTS

MUST DOs

MUST DOs

☐

☐

☐

☐

Weekly Planner

Date: _____

TO DO	SPECIAL EVENT

APPOINTMENTS	THINGS TO BUY

REMINDERS	NEED TO CALL

REMARKS

MONDAY

9:00 AM	4:00 PM
10:00 AM	5:00 PM
11:00 AM	6:00 PM
12:00 PM	MUST DOs
1:00 PM	☐
2:00 PM	☐
3:00 PM	☐

TUESDAY

9:00 AM	4:00 PM
10:00 AM	5:00 PM
11:00 AM	6:00 PM
12:00 PM	MUST DOs
1:00 PM	☐
2:00 PM	☐
3:00 PM	☐

WEDNESDAY

9:00 AM	4:00 PM
10:00 AM	5:00 PM
11:00 AM	6:00 PM
12:00 PM	MUST DOs
1:00 PM	☐
2:00 PM	☐
3:00 PM	☐

THURSDAY

9:00 AM	4:00 PM
10:00 AM	5:00 PM
11:00 AM	6:00 PM
12:00 PM	MUST DOs
1:00 PM	☐
2:00 PM	☐
3:00 PM	☐

FRIDAY

9:00 AM	4:00 PM
10:00 AM	5:00 PM
11:00 AM	6:00 PM
12:00 PM	MUST DOs
1:00 PM	☐
2:00 PM	☐
3:00 PM	☐

SATURDAY
APPOINTMENTS

SUNDAY
APPOINTMENTS

MUST DOs	MUST DOs
☐	☐
☐	☐

Weekly Planner

Date: _____

TO DO	SPECIAL EVENT

APPOINTMENTS	THINGS TO BUY

REMINDERS	NEED TO CALL

REMARKS

MONDAY

9:00 AM	4:00 PM
10:00 AM	5:00 PM
11:00 AM	6:00 PM
12:00 PM	MUST DOs
1:00 PM	☐
2:00 PM	☐
3:00 PM	☐

TUESDAY

9:00 AM	4:00 PM
10:00 AM	5:00 PM
11:00 AM	6:00 PM
12:00 PM	MUST DOs
1:00 PM	☐
2:00 PM	☐
3:00 PM	☐

WEDNESDAY

9:00 AM	4:00 PM
10:00 AM	5:00 PM
11:00 AM	6:00 PM
12:00 PM	MUST DOs
1:00 PM	☐
2:00 PM	☐
3:00 PM	☐

THURSDAY

9:00 AM	4:00 PM
10:00 AM	5:00 PM
11:00 AM	6:00 PM
12:00 PM	MUST DOs
1:00 PM	☐
2:00 PM	☐
3:00 PM	☐

FRIDAY

9:00 AM	4:00 PM
10:00 AM	5:00 PM
11:00 AM	6:00 PM
12:00 PM	MUST DOs
1:00 PM	☐
2:00 PM	☐
3:00 PM	☐

SATURDAY

APPOINTMENTS

MUST DOs

☐
☐

SUNDAY

APPOINTMENTS

MUST DOs

☐
☐

Weekly Planner

Date: _____

TO DO

SPECIAL EVENT

APPOINTMENTS

THINGS TO BUY

REMINDERS

NEED TO CALL

REMARKS

MONDAY

9:00 AM	4:00 PM
10:00 AM	5:00 PM
11:00 AM	6:00 PM
12:00 PM	MUST DOs
1:00 PM	☐
2:00 PM	☐
3:00 PM	☐

TUESDAY

9:00 AM	4:00 PM
10:00 AM	5:00 PM
11:00 AM	6:00 PM
12:00 PM	MUST DOs
1:00 PM	☐
2:00 PM	☐
3:00 PM	☐

WEDNESDAY

9:00 AM	4:00 PM
10:00 AM	5:00 PM
11:00 AM	6:00 PM
12:00 PM	MUST DOs
1:00 PM	☐
2:00 PM	☐
3:00 PM	☐

THURSDAY

9:00 AM	4:00 PM
10:00 AM	5:00 PM
11:00 AM	6:00 PM
12:00 PM	MUST DOs
1:00 PM	☐
2:00 PM	☐
3:00 PM	☐

FRIDAY

9:00 AM	4:00 PM
10:00 AM	5:00 PM
11:00 AM	6:00 PM
12:00 PM	MUST DOs
1:00 PM	☐
2:00 PM	☐
3:00 PM	☐

SATURDAY
APPOINTMENTS

SUNDAY
APPOINTMENTS

MUST DOs

☐

☐

MUST DOs

☐

☐

Weekly Planner
Date: _____

TO DO

SPECIAL EVENT

APPOINTMENTS

THINGS TO BUY

REMINDERS

NEED TO CALL

REMARKS

MONDAY

9:00 AM	4:00 PM
10:00 AM	5:00 PM
11:00 AM	6:00 PM
12:00 PM	MUST DOs
1:00 PM	☐
2:00 PM	☐
3:00 PM	☐

TUESDAY

9:00 AM	4:00 PM
10:00 AM	5:00 PM
11:00 AM	6:00 PM
12:00 PM	MUST DOs
1:00 PM	☐
2:00 PM	☐
3:00 PM	☐

WEDNESDAY

9:00 AM	4:00 PM
10:00 AM	5:00 PM
11:00 AM	6:00 PM
12:00 PM	MUST DOs
1:00 PM	☐
2:00 PM	☐
3:00 PM	☐

THURSDAY

9:00 AM	4:00 PM
10:00 AM	5:00 PM
11:00 AM	6:00 PM
12:00 PM	MUST DOs
1:00 PM	☐
2:00 PM	☐
3:00 PM	☐

FRIDAY

9:00 AM	4:00 PM
10:00 AM	5:00 PM
11:00 AM	6:00 PM
12:00 PM	MUST DOs
1:00 PM	☐
2:00 PM	☐
3:00 PM	☐

SATURDAY
APPOINTMENTS

SUNDAY
APPOINTMENTS

MUST DOs

☐

☐

MUST DOs

☐

☐

Weekly Planner
Date: _____

TO DO

SPECIAL EVENT

APPOINTMENTS

THINGS TO BUY

REMINDERS

NEED TO CALL

REMARKS

MONDAY

9:00 AM	4:00 PM
10:00 AM	5:00 PM
11:00 AM	6:00 PM
12:00 PM	MUST DOs
1:00 PM	☐
2:00 PM	☐
3:00 PM	☐

TUESDAY

9:00 AM	4:00 PM
10:00 AM	5:00 PM
11:00 AM	6:00 PM
12:00 PM	MUST DOs
1:00 PM	☐
2:00 PM	☐
3:00 PM	☐

WEDNESDAY

9:00 AM	4:00 PM
10:00 AM	5:00 PM
11:00 AM	6:00 PM
12:00 PM	MUST DOs
1:00 PM	☐
2:00 PM	☐
3:00 PM	☐

THURSDAY

9:00 AM	4:00 PM
10:00 AM	5:00 PM
11:00 AM	6:00 PM
12:00 PM	MUST DOs
1:00 PM	☐
2:00 PM	☐
3:00 PM	☐

FRIDAY

9:00 AM	4:00 PM
10:00 AM	5:00 PM
11:00 AM	6:00 PM
12:00 PM	MUST DOs
1:00 PM	☐
2:00 PM	☐
3:00 PM	☐

SATURDAY
APPOINTMENTS

SUNDAY
APPOINTMENTS

MUST DOs

☐

☐

MUST DOs

☐

☐

Weekly Planner
Date: _____

TO DO

SPECIAL EVENT

APPOINTMENTS

THINGS TO BUY

REMINDERS

NEED TO CALL

REMARKS

MONDAY

9:00 AM	4:00 PM
10:00 AM	5:00 PM
11:00 AM	6:00 PM
12:00 PM	MUST DOs
1:00 PM	☐
2:00 PM	☐
3:00 PM	☐

TUESDAY

9:00 AM	4:00 PM
10:00 AM	5:00 PM
11:00 AM	6:00 PM
12:00 PM	MUST DOs
1:00 PM	☐
2:00 PM	☐
3:00 PM	☐

WEDNESDAY

9:00 AM	4:00 PM
10:00 AM	5:00 PM
11:00 AM	6:00 PM
12:00 PM	MUST DOs
1:00 PM	☐
2:00 PM	☐
3:00 PM	☐

THURSDAY

9:00 AM	4:00 PM
10:00 AM	5:00 PM
11:00 AM	6:00 PM
12:00 PM	MUST DOs
1:00 PM	☐
2:00 PM	☐
3:00 PM	☐

FRIDAY

9:00 AM	4:00 PM
10:00 AM	5:00 PM
11:00 AM	6:00 PM
12:00 PM	MUST DOs
1:00 PM	☐
2:00 PM	☐
3:00 PM	☐

SATURDAY
APPOINTMENTS

SUNDAY
APPOINTMENTS

MUST DOs

☐
☐

MUST DOs

☐
☐

Weekly Planner

Date: _____

TO DO	SPECIAL EVENT

APPOINTMENTS	THINGS TO BUY

REMINDERS	NEED TO CALL

REMARKS

MONDAY

9:00 AM	4:00 PM
10:00 AM	5:00 PM
11:00 AM	6:00 PM
12:00 PM	MUST DOs
1:00 PM	☐
2:00 PM	☐
3:00 PM	☐

TUESDAY

9:00 AM	4:00 PM
10:00 AM	5:00 PM
11:00 AM	6:00 PM
12:00 PM	MUST DOs
1:00 PM	☐
2:00 PM	☐
3:00 PM	☐

WEDNESDAY

9:00 AM	4:00 PM
10:00 AM	5:00 PM
11:00 AM	6:00 PM
12:00 PM	MUST DOs
1:00 PM	☐
2:00 PM	☐
3:00 PM	☐

THURSDAY

9:00 AM	4:00 PM
10:00 AM	5:00 PM
11:00 AM	6:00 PM
12:00 PM	MUST DOs
1:00 PM	☐
2:00 PM	☐
3:00 PM	☐

FRIDAY

9:00 AM	4:00 PM
10:00 AM	5:00 PM
11:00 AM	6:00 PM
12:00 PM	MUST DOs
1:00 PM	☐
2:00 PM	☐
3:00 PM	☐

SATURDAY
APPOINTMENTS

SUNDAY
APPOINTMENTS

MUST DOs
☐
☐

MUST DOs
☐
☐

Weekly Planner

Date: _____

TO DO	SPECIAL EVENT

APPOINTMENTS	THINGS TO BUY

REMINDERS	NEED TO CALL

REMARKS

MONDAY

9:00 AM	4:00 PM
10:00 AM	5:00 PM
11:00 AM	6:00 PM
12:00 PM	MUST DOs
1:00 PM	☐
2:00 PM	☐
3:00 PM	☐

TUESDAY

9:00 AM	4:00 PM
10:00 AM	5:00 PM
11:00 AM	6:00 PM
12:00 PM	MUST DOs
1:00 PM	☐
2:00 PM	☐
3:00 PM	☐

WEDNESDAY

9:00 AM	4:00 PM
10:00 AM	5:00 PM
11:00 AM	6:00 PM
12:00 PM	MUST DOs
1:00 PM	☐
2:00 PM	☐
3:00 PM	☐

THURSDAY

9:00 AM	4:00 PM
10:00 AM	5:00 PM
11:00 AM	6:00 PM
12:00 PM	MUST DOs
1:00 PM	☐
2:00 PM	☐
3:00 PM	☐

FRIDAY

9:00 AM	4:00 PM
10:00 AM	5:00 PM
11:00 AM	6:00 PM
12:00 PM	MUST DOs
1:00 PM	☐
2:00 PM	☐
3:00 PM	☐

SATURDAY
APPOINTMENTS

SUNDAY
APPOINTMENTS

MUST DOs

☐

☐

MUST DOs

☐

☐

Weekly Planner

Date: _____

TO DO	SPECIAL EVENT

APPOINTMENTS	THINGS TO BUY

REMINDERS	NEED TO CALL

REMARKS

MONDAY

9:00 AM	4:00 PM
10:00 AM	5:00 PM
11:00 AM	6:00 PM
12:00 PM	MUST DOs
1:00 PM	☐
2:00 PM	☐
3:00 PM	☐

TUESDAY

9:00 AM	4:00 PM
10:00 AM	5:00 PM
11:00 AM	6:00 PM
12:00 PM	MUST DOs
1:00 PM	☐
2:00 PM	☐
3:00 PM	☐

WEDNESDAY

9:00 AM	4:00 PM
10:00 AM	5:00 PM
11:00 AM	6:00 PM
12:00 PM	MUST DOs
1:00 PM	☐
2:00 PM	☐
3:00 PM	☐

THURSDAY

9:00 AM	4:00 PM
10:00 AM	5:00 PM
11:00 AM	6:00 PM
12:00 PM	MUST DOs
1:00 PM	☐
2:00 PM	☐
3:00 PM	☐

FRIDAY

9:00 AM	4:00 PM
10:00 AM	5:00 PM
11:00 AM	6:00 PM
12:00 PM	MUST DOs
1:00 PM	☐
2:00 PM	☐
3:00 PM	☐

SATURDAY
APPOINTMENTS

SUNDAY
APPOINTMENTS

MUST DOs

☐

☐

MUST DOs

☐

☐

Weekly Planner

Date: _____

TO DO

SPECIAL EVENT

APPOINTMENTS

THINGS TO BUY

REMINDERS

NEED TO CALL

REMARKS

MONDAY

9:00 AM	4:00 PM
10:00 AM	5:00 PM
11:00 AM	6:00 PM
12:00 PM	MUST DOs
1:00 PM	☐
2:00 PM	☐
3:00 PM	☐

TUESDAY

9:00 AM	4:00 PM
10:00 AM	5:00 PM
11:00 AM	6:00 PM
12:00 PM	MUST DOs
1:00 PM	☐
2:00 PM	☐
3:00 PM	☐

WEDNESDAY

9:00 AM	4:00 PM
10:00 AM	5:00 PM
11:00 AM	6:00 PM
12:00 PM	MUST DOs
1:00 PM	☐
2:00 PM	☐
3:00 PM	☐

THURSDAY

9:00 AM	4:00 PM
10:00 AM	5:00 PM
11:00 AM	6:00 PM
12:00 PM	MUST DOs
1:00 PM	☐
2:00 PM	☐
3:00 PM	☐

FRIDAY

9:00 AM	4:00 PM
10:00 AM	5:00 PM
11:00 AM	6:00 PM
12:00 PM	MUST DOs
1:00 PM	☐
2:00 PM	☐
3:00 PM	☐

SATURDAY
APPOINTMENTS

SUNDAY
APPOINTMENTS

MUST DOs

☐
☐

MUST DOs

☐
☐

Weekly Planner

Date: _____

TO DO

SPECIAL EVENT

APPOINTMENTS

THINGS TO BUY

REMINDERS

NEED TO CALL

REMARKS

MONDAY

9:00 AM	4:00 PM
10:00 AM	5:00 PM
11:00 AM	6:00 PM
12:00 PM	MUST DOs
1:00 PM	☐
2:00 PM	☐
3:00 PM	☐

TUESDAY

9:00 AM	4:00 PM
10:00 AM	5:00 PM
11:00 AM	6:00 PM
12:00 PM	MUST DOs
1:00 PM	☐
2:00 PM	☐
3:00 PM	☐

WEDNESDAY

9:00 AM	4:00 PM
10:00 AM	5:00 PM
11:00 AM	6:00 PM
12:00 PM	MUST DOs
1:00 PM	☐
2:00 PM	☐
3:00 PM	☐

THURSDAY

9:00 AM	4:00 PM
10:00 AM	5:00 PM
11:00 AM	6:00 PM
12:00 PM	MUST DOs
1:00 PM	☐
2:00 PM	☐
3:00 PM	☐

FRIDAY

9:00 AM	4:00 PM
10:00 AM	5:00 PM
11:00 AM	6:00 PM
12:00 PM	MUST DOs
1:00 PM	☐
2:00 PM	☐
3:00 PM	☐

SATURDAY
APPOINTMENTS

SUNDAY
APPOINTMENTS

MUST DOs

☐

☐

MUST DOs

☐

☐

Weekly Planner

Date: _____

TO DO

SPECIAL EVENT

APPOINTMENTS

THINGS TO BUY

REMINDERS

NEED TO CALL

REMARKS

MONDAY

9:00 AM	4:00 PM
10:00 AM	5:00 PM
11:00 AM	6:00 PM
12:00 PM	MUST DOs
1:00 PM	☐
2:00 PM	☐
3:00 PM	☐

TUESDAY

9:00 AM	4:00 PM
10:00 AM	5:00 PM
11:00 AM	6:00 PM
12:00 PM	MUST DOs
1:00 PM	☐
2:00 PM	☐
3:00 PM	☐

WEDNESDAY

9:00 AM	4:00 PM
10:00 AM	5:00 PM
11:00 AM	6:00 PM
12:00 PM	MUST DOs
1:00 PM	☐
2:00 PM	☐
3:00 PM	☐

THURSDAY

9:00 AM	4:00 PM
10:00 AM	5:00 PM
11:00 AM	6:00 PM
12:00 PM	MUST DOs
1:00 PM	☐
2:00 PM	☐
3:00 PM	☐

FRIDAY

9:00 AM	4:00 PM
10:00 AM	5:00 PM
11:00 AM	6:00 PM
12:00 PM	MUST DOs
1:00 PM	☐
2:00 PM	☐
3:00 PM	☐

SATURDAY
APPOINTMENTS

SUNDAY
APPOINTMENTS

MUST DOs

☐

☐

MUST DOs

☐

☐

Weekly Planner

Date: _____

TO DO	SPECIAL EVENT

APPOINTMENTS	THINGS TO BUY

REMINDERS	NEED TO CALL

REMARKS

MONDAY

9:00 AM	4:00 PM
10:00 AM	5:00 PM
11:00 AM	6:00 PM
12:00 PM	MUST DOs
1:00 PM	☐
2:00 PM	☐
3:00 PM	☐

TUESDAY

9:00 AM	4:00 PM
10:00 AM	5:00 PM
11:00 AM	6:00 PM
12:00 PM	MUST DOs
1:00 PM	☐
2:00 PM	☐
3:00 PM	☐

WEDNESDAY

9:00 AM	4:00 PM
10:00 AM	5:00 PM
11:00 AM	6:00 PM
12:00 PM	MUST DOs
1:00 PM	☐
2:00 PM	☐
3:00 PM	☐

THURSDAY

9:00 AM	4:00 PM
10:00 AM	5:00 PM
11:00 AM	6:00 PM
12:00 PM	MUST DOs
1:00 PM	☐
2:00 PM	☐
3:00 PM	☐

FRIDAY

9:00 AM	4:00 PM
10:00 AM	5:00 PM
11:00 AM	6:00 PM
12:00 PM	MUST DOs
1:00 PM	☐
2:00 PM	☐
3:00 PM	☐

SATURDAY
APPOINTMENTS

SUNDAY
APPOINTMENTS

MUST DOs

☐
☐

MUST DOs

☐
☐

Weekly Planner
Date: _____

TO DO

SPECIAL EVENT

APPOINTMENTS

THINGS TO BUY

REMINDERS

NEED TO CALL

REMARKS

MONDAY

9:00 AM	4:00 PM
10:00 AM	5:00 PM
11:00 AM	6:00 PM
12:00 PM	MUST DOs
1:00 PM	☐
2:00 PM	☐
3:00 PM	☐

TUESDAY

9:00 AM	4:00 PM
10:00 AM	5:00 PM
11:00 AM	6:00 PM
12:00 PM	MUST DOs
1:00 PM	☐
2:00 PM	☐
3:00 PM	☐

WEDNESDAY

9:00 AM	4:00 PM
10:00 AM	5:00 PM
11:00 AM	6:00 PM
12:00 PM	MUST DOs
1:00 PM	☐
2:00 PM	☐
3:00 PM	☐

THURSDAY

9:00 AM	4:00 PM
10:00 AM	5:00 PM
11:00 AM	6:00 PM
12:00 PM	MUST DOs
1:00 PM	☐
2:00 PM	☐
3:00 PM	☐

FRIDAY

9:00 AM	4:00 PM
10:00 AM	5:00 PM
11:00 AM	6:00 PM
12:00 PM	MUST DOs
1:00 PM	☐
2:00 PM	☐
3:00 PM	☐

SATURDAY
APPOINTMENTS

SUNDAY
APPOINTMENTS

MUST DOs

☐
☐

MUST DOs

☐
☐

Weekly Planner
Date: _____

TO DO

SPECIAL EVENT

APPOINTMENTS

THINGS TO BUY

REMINDERS

NEED TO CALL

REMARKS

MONDAY

9:00 AM	4:00 PM
10:00 AM	5:00 PM
11:00 AM	6:00 PM
12:00 PM	MUST DOs
1:00 PM	☐
2:00 PM	☐
3:00 PM	☐

TUESDAY

9:00 AM	4:00 PM
10:00 AM	5:00 PM
11:00 AM	6:00 PM
12:00 PM	MUST DOs
1:00 PM	☐
2:00 PM	☐
3:00 PM	☐

WEDNESDAY

9:00 AM	4:00 PM
10:00 AM	5:00 PM
11:00 AM	6:00 PM
12:00 PM	MUST DOs
1:00 PM	☐
2:00 PM	☐
3:00 PM	☐

THURSDAY

9:00 AM	4:00 PM
10:00 AM	5:00 PM
11:00 AM	6:00 PM
12:00 PM	MUST DOs
1:00 PM	☐
2:00 PM	☐
3:00 PM	☐

FRIDAY

9:00 AM	4:00 PM
10:00 AM	5:00 PM
11:00 AM	6:00 PM
12:00 PM	MUST DOs
1:00 PM	☐
2:00 PM	☐
3:00 PM	☐

SATURDAY
APPOINTMENTS

SUNDAY
APPOINTMENTS

MUST DOs

☐

☐

MUST DOs

☐

☐

Weekly Planner

Date: _____

TO DO	SPECIAL EVENT

APPOINTMENTS	THINGS TO BUY

REMINDERS	NEED TO CALL

REMARKS

MONDAY

9:00 AM	4:00 PM
10:00 AM	5:00 PM
11:00 AM	6:00 PM
12:00 PM	MUST DOs
1:00 PM	☐
2:00 PM	☐
3:00 PM	☐

TUESDAY

9:00 AM	4:00 PM
10:00 AM	5:00 PM
11:00 AM	6:00 PM
12:00 PM	MUST DOs
1:00 PM	☐
2:00 PM	☐
3:00 PM	☐

WEDNESDAY

9:00 AM	4:00 PM
10:00 AM	5:00 PM
11:00 AM	6:00 PM
12:00 PM	MUST DOs
1:00 PM	☐
2:00 PM	☐
3:00 PM	☐

THURSDAY

9:00 AM	4:00 PM
10:00 AM	5:00 PM
11:00 AM	6:00 PM
12:00 PM	MUST DOs
1:00 PM	☐
2:00 PM	☐
3:00 PM	☐

FRIDAY

9:00 AM	4:00 PM
10:00 AM	5:00 PM
11:00 AM	6:00 PM
12:00 PM	MUST DOs
1:00 PM	☐
2:00 PM	☐
3:00 PM	☐

SATURDAY
APPOINTMENTS

SUNDAY
APPOINTMENTS

MUST DOs

☐

☐

MUST DOs

☐

☐

Weekly Planner
Date: _____

TO DO	SPECIAL EVENT

APPOINTMENTS	THINGS TO BUY

REMINDERS	NEED TO CALL

REMARKS

MONDAY

9:00 AM	4:00 PM
10:00 AM	5:00 PM
11:00 AM	6:00 PM
12:00 PM	MUST DOs
1:00 PM	☐
2:00 PM	☐
3:00 PM	☐

TUESDAY

9:00 AM	4:00 PM
10:00 AM	5:00 PM
11:00 AM	6:00 PM
12:00 PM	MUST DOs
1:00 PM	☐
2:00 PM	☐
3:00 PM	☐

WEDNESDAY

9:00 AM	4:00 PM
10:00 AM	5:00 PM
11:00 AM	6:00 PM
12:00 PM	MUST DOs
1:00 PM	☐
2:00 PM	☐
3:00 PM	☐

THURSDAY

9:00 AM	4:00 PM
10:00 AM	5:00 PM
11:00 AM	6:00 PM
12:00 PM	MUST DOs
1:00 PM	☐
2:00 PM	☐
3:00 PM	☐

FRIDAY

9:00 AM	4:00 PM
10:00 AM	5:00 PM
11:00 AM	6:00 PM
12:00 PM	MUST DOs
1:00 PM	☐
2:00 PM	☐
3:00 PM	☐

SATURDAY
APPOINTMENTS

SUNDAY
APPOINTMENTS

MUST DOs

☐
☐

MUST DOs

☐
☐

Weekly Planner

Date: _____

TO DO	SPECIAL EVENT

APPOINTMENTS	THINGS TO BUY

REMINDERS	NEED TO CALL

REMARKS

MONDAY

9:00 AM	4:00 PM
10:00 AM	5:00 PM
11:00 AM	6:00 PM
12:00 PM	MUST DOs
1:00 PM	☐
2:00 PM	☐
3:00 PM	☐

TUESDAY

9:00 AM	4:00 PM
10:00 AM	5:00 PM
11:00 AM	6:00 PM
12:00 PM	MUST DOs
1:00 PM	☐
2:00 PM	☐
3:00 PM	☐

WEDNESDAY

9:00 AM	4:00 PM
10:00 AM	5:00 PM
11:00 AM	6:00 PM
12:00 PM	MUST DOs
1:00 PM	☐
2:00 PM	☐
3:00 PM	☐

THURSDAY

9:00 AM	4:00 PM
10:00 AM	5:00 PM
11:00 AM	6:00 PM
12:00 PM	MUST DOs
1:00 PM	☐
2:00 PM	☐
3:00 PM	☐

FRIDAY

9:00 AM	4:00 PM
10:00 AM	5:00 PM
11:00 AM	6:00 PM
12:00 PM	MUST DOs
1:00 PM	☐
2:00 PM	☐
3:00 PM	☐

SATURDAY

APPOINTMENTS

SUNDAY

APPOINTMENTS

MUST DOs

☐
☐

MUST DOs

☐
☐

Weekly Planner
Date: _____

TO DO	SPECIAL EVENT

APPOINTMENTS	THINGS TO BUY

REMINDERS	NEED TO CALL

REMARKS

MONDAY

9:00 AM	4:00 PM
10:00 AM	5:00 PM
11:00 AM	6:00 PM
12:00 PM	MUST DOs
1:00 PM	☐
2:00 PM	☐
3:00 PM	☐

TUESDAY

9:00 AM	4:00 PM
10:00 AM	5:00 PM
11:00 AM	6:00 PM
12:00 PM	MUST DOs
1:00 PM	☐
2:00 PM	☐
3:00 PM	☐

WEDNESDAY

9:00 AM	4:00 PM
10:00 AM	5:00 PM
11:00 AM	6:00 PM
12:00 PM	MUST DOs
1:00 PM	☐
2:00 PM	☐
3:00 PM	☐

THURSDAY

9:00 AM	4:00 PM
10:00 AM	5:00 PM
11:00 AM	6:00 PM
12:00 PM	MUST DOs
1:00 PM	☐
2:00 PM	☐
3:00 PM	☐

FRIDAY

9:00 AM	4:00 PM
10:00 AM	5:00 PM
11:00 AM	6:00 PM
12:00 PM	MUST DOs
1:00 PM	☐
2:00 PM	☐
3:00 PM	☐

SATURDAY
APPOINTMENTS

SUNDAY
APPOINTMENTS

MUST DOs

☐

☐

MUST DOs

☐

☐

Weekly Planner

Date: _____

TO DO

SPECIAL EVENT

APPOINTMENTS

THINGS TO BUY

REMINDERS

NEED TO CALL

REMARKS

www.ingramcontent.com/pod-product-compliance
Lightning Source LLC
Chambersburg PA
CBHW081336090426

42737CB00017B/3172